THIS BOOK
BELONGS TO

_____

DATE

DATE

DATE

DATE

DATE

DATE

DATE

DATE

DATE

DATE

DATE

DATE

DATE

DATE

DATE

DATE

DATE

DATE

DATE

DATE

DATE

DATE

DATE

DATE

DATE

DATE

DATE

DATE

DATE

DATE

DATE

DATE

DATE

DATE

DATE

DATE

DATE

DATE

DATE

DATE

DATE

DATE

DATE

DATE

DATE

DATE

DATE

DATE

DATE

DATE

DATE

DATE

DATE

DATE

DATE

DATE

DATE

DATE

DATE

DATE

DATE

DATE

DATE

DATE

Made in the USA
Monee, IL
19 December 2021

86482609R00083